# Contents

# Introduction

In 2011, I was invited to teach a course at Fuller Seminary called ST511 Orientation to Theological Studies. The course was a requirement for students who were accepted to Fuller on a probationary status. Maybe they had low grades, or didn't finish their undergraduate degree, or some other reason. The main goal was to teach writing and research skills. I adapted it to be more of an introduction to the main topics in seminary with the writing and research skills developed through exercises along the way. We spent a couple weeks focused on Biblical Studies, a couple weeks focused on theology, a couple weeks focused on church history, and a couple weeks focused on ministry. Each week I also wrote a short reflection on an issue or theme related to the exercises, the topics, or general seminary issues (like navigating seminary faith challenges or how to read a book). This present text is a collection of those reflections.

As I continue to teach for Fuller, it really is my passion to help students navigate learning the content in a holistic way, encouraging and guiding them to become better learners, to discover their calling, to sharpen their skills, and to do this in a way that allows them to still have a fruitful life outside of seminary studies. That's not an easy task. But it is possible. These reflections draw on my own experiences as a seminary student and as a teacher of seminary students.

I hope you find this guide useful in part or as a whole.

# Writing in Seminary

People come to seminary for all sorts of reasons. They feel a call to ministry. They have questions about God that no one they know can answer. They're interested in studying more about God, the Bible or the history of the church. Very few people go to seminary because they want to be a better writer. But the fact is that once you're in seminary, for whatever reason you have for being there, you will be asked to do two tasks more than just about anything else.

You will have to read and you will have to write.

Indeed, you will have to read probably more than you've ever read before in the amount of time you are given. Almost certainly, you will have to write more than you've ever written before, on topics which you may know little about, and often must research topics that you know nothing about.

That sounds like a lot of work. It is.

But it is also an opportunity. Because you get the chance to learn how to better understand the Bible, Christian history, theology, and all the various tasks that are involved in ministry. If you use this time to your advantage, you will finish seminary able to contribute a significant amount of depth and an enlightening perspective to people who may not have other sources of reliable information about God.

So, plan to read a lot and plan to write. You will do both a lot so you might as well plan how to do these with the best possible result.

Of these two, writing may be the more important task because your grades in seminary are, for just about every class, dependent on what you write. And if you know how to write well, you will know how to read better. Writing causes you to be more aware of what you are reading and more aware of how other writers are organizing their information. That is why you will write a fair number of book reviews or short responses about readings during your time in graduate school. Writing about a book makes you think about it more than merely reading it, and knowing you have to write about it makes you read a book more attentively.

The trouble is that far too many students do not know how to write. I'm not saying they're illiterate. Most everyone in our present society can write a grocery list or send an email. Indeed, to get into seminary, or other graduate schools, most people have attended college where essays were required in at least some classes. Even those whose path to seminary has been nontraditional, they have learned to write in high school, in business situations, in churches, or elsewhere. People, for the most part, know how to put words on paper in some kind of understandable order.

Few people know how to write well.

Writing well is the difference between an A and a B, and sometimes even the difference between a B and a C. It's the difference between convincing someone of your argument and confusing them even more. It's the difference between compiling something that might be helpful later and something that you'll never look at or think about again. Good writing covers a multitude of sins, meaning that if you're a good writer you can be more convincing and get better grades than a smarter, harder working fellow student who happens to be merely an adequate writer.

Now if your goal is just to get a few letters after your name, to get through the hoops of ordination or to impress your neighbors and friends, then you can probably get by in seminary or other graduate programs by writing merely adequate assignments. But is that enough? Your time in seminary, or whatever higher education you pursue, is a great opportunity that the majority of people in this world, and the great number of people throughout history, won't get. Moreover, you are studying what some consider the most important topics of all. That is worth a bit more care, I think.

You can get by, or you can take advantage of this opportunity to learn skills and knowledge that will help you for the rest of your life. Not that long term of a thinker? Well, learn skills that will help you right away.

Learning how to write well is one of these skills. Because if you write well you can communicate to people in a way that helps them. You can lead others through discussion passages in the Bible, helping them understand what might seem to be complicated notions of theology. Or, you can help the downcast find hope and truth during times of personal struggle. Knowing how to write well helps you organize your thoughts. That organization shapes not only how you write but also how you speak.

Have I convinced you yet? Hopefully, because I have a lot more to say.

My hope is also to help you learn how to continue to improve your writing skills and maybe even learn how to enjoy writing. I want you to learn how to write better and I want to inspire you about the value of writing, to inspire you about the value of your writing. You have something to say, after all. I have no doubt about that. So you might as well learn how to say it in the best way possible.

Even if I don't inspire you to love writing more and can't convince you how important it is to life outside of graduate school, I hope to at least help your teachers, their assistants, and anyone else who might read what you write. As someone who has graded many papers and will, no doubt, grade many, many more I have to confess my selfish interest. I am tired of reading bad papers. Reading bad papers is frustrating because bad writing gives me more work, and when I have a lot of students and many papers to grade I already am lacking for enough time to read every paper thoroughly.

Bad writing gives me more work because I have to sort out what the writer is trying to say, and I have to sort out what the writer is trying to do, and I then, as the person grading, have to explain why the grade is lower than might have been expected. I don't want to read bad writing and I hope you don't want to turn in bad writing. Fortunately, it's not too difficult to start on the path to good writing skills.

# Practicing Writing

You might be wondering why classes have so many forums. Online classes seem to rely on forums and increasingly even classroom based courses use forums. Here are some reasons I use them:

I use forums in my online classes as a way of getting students to engage each other.

A second reason is that I want students to engage the material. It is very easy to do the bare minimum or much less than the bare minimum in classes like these, so forums are my way of encouraging students to do the work and think about the work. Forums are a great way to check if the students are doing the readings.

There's another reason. I want students to write. I want my students to get used to writing and the only way a person gets used to writing is by writing.

Writing is a lot like jogging or other exercise. You can read books about jogging. You can buy nice shoes and running shorts, and even an armband to hold your ipod. You can spend an immense amount of time watching people run. But unless you actually go running, you won't be able to run farther or faster.

The only way to learn how to write better is by writing.

Writing by itself doesn't always help, we often need motivation and guidance in our writing. That's why we write so much in classes.

I want you to also notice how the authors of the books you are reading are writing. Notice how they arrange things. Notice how they emphasize key points. Notice how and where they summarize. Notice how they argue and develop concepts. All these things are important to notice.

But, again, the key to writing is writing. If you haven't written a long bit of text in while, it can seem difficult to compose your thoughts and put together a research paper. But if you're writing a lot, you'll find your thoughts coming together as you write.

So, I encourage students to use forums as a way of stretching their writing endurance. Other ways of practicing writing include blogs, or journaling, or writing to someone who might appreciate substantive interaction.

Write? Of course, write.

# Citing Sources

There are many online resources to help you properly cite your sources, but I thought it would be helpful to give some very basic guidelines.

- Here's what you'll always need for a book:
  - Author
  - Title
  - Publisher
  - City of Publication
  - Year of Publication
- Here's what you'll always need for an article:
  - Author
  - Title of Article
  - Journal Title
  - Issue #
  - Page(s)

The order these go in is generally always the same, but you'll arrange them differently depending on whether you are citing in a footnote or citing in a bibliography. **A bibliography citation looks different than a footnote citation.** For instance, in a bibliography the last name goes first, then the first name follows. In a footnote, the first name is first and then the last name. Also, in a bibliography there are a lot of periods. In a footnote, there are more commas. There are other differences.

Until you have the citation style memorized, always double check. You can look online for lists as well. You can also buy books on this, but since most everything you need to know is found online, there's probably no reason to spend the money unless you are planning to stay in academia. Books like

*Turabian Made Easy!* have the most common styles and offer helpful tips for structure and style. I have Turabian's *A Manual for Writers* as well as the more comprehensive *Chicago Manual of Style*. However, when I have a question I still generally just look online.

Turabian and the Chicago Style are pretty much the same. So, if someone says Chicago Style, feel comfortable using Turabian. Turabian is basically more streamlined and focused and contained in a much smaller, much lighter book. But it is based on Chicago Style.

Again, you need at the very least those elements I mentioned above, sometimes more depending on what you are citing. You cannot, however, just put these elements in any order you want. There is a precise style that you must follow for everything you cite.

Let me correct what I just said. You will always need those elements above, and sometimes more, only when you first cite a book or article or other source. After you first give the full information you don't need to write all that again. Just the last name of the author and the page number (for example: Oden, 265). If you are using more than one book or source by the same person, give the title after the last name (for example: Oden, *It's a Dance*, 244).

Another big tip is to ask if you have other questions or issues. This may all seem like busy work or minutiae, but it's part of participating in the field, so the sooner you get comfortable with it all, the easier it is, and you'll avoid losing points on papers. And professors and TAs appreciate when students ask about such things. It means they care!

# Spiritual Life while in Seminary

Over the course of your time at Fuller, you will study a whole lot of Scripture, think about God's identity and work in this world, consider the practices and history of the church, and otherwise be very intensely engaged in topics relating to ministry and theology.

Following a long standing approach to seminary education, now under reconsideration at Fuller and elsewhere, this is primarily an intellectual pursuit. We read a lot of books, write papers using words with multiple syllables, and discuss key tactics and debates using the height of our rational thinking skills.

This approach would be entirely fitting if we were Vulcans but it has particular weaknesses for most people. We do not nicely separate our intellectual from our emotional from our spiritual sides. Nor should we neatly separate these, as they often inform each other.

This approach to seminary does not necessarily insist on doing this, but it does tend to compartmentalize the intellectual from the spiritual. In the Modern model of education, seminary teaches the facts, the skills, that are required in pastoral ministry or advanced theological education. Other aspects were assumed to be taken care of by a church or other such places.

The trouble is that by compartmentalizing, a seminary education often leads to men and women who are disjointed, discouraged, frustrated, not knowing how to integrate their growing knowledge with their personal experiences.

Some people are so busy while in seminary they don't notice. But it catches up with them eventually. That's why most seminary students encounter a spiritual crisis in one form or another. Sometimes that directed inwardly as a crisis of faith. Sometimes that's directed outwardly against others.

One way or another, it is almost guaranteed that seminary will cause some disturbances in your spiritual, emotional, and intellectual life. This is especially the case if a lot of the material is new to you, but even if is familiar, it will shake things up in how you view the world.

So how do we process all this? That's where an intentional response on your part becomes so important. If you encounter all this new information in the context of a thriving spiritual life, you will be able to process it much more helpfully, helpfully to yourself and helpfully for others.

Right at the beginning of seminary is a great time to think about ways in which you can develop or maintain habits that make sure that while you're studying a lot about God you're growing in your relationship with him.

**If you are a theologian, you will pray truly. And if you pray truly, you are a theologian.**
**~ Evagrios of Pontus**

Traditionally, an organized pattern to the sort of spiritual disciplines that will help you along the way of spiritual maturity and stability is called a Rule. There are many, many different examples of these throughout history, the most famous one probably being the Rule of St. Benedict, which was designed to help organize communities of men and women.

These sorts of rules aren't laws that must be followed to achieve salvation. They're more like commitments we make to spiritual practices that will help us focus and mature. They can be agreed upon by communities or created for individual use.

**"If you are a theologian, you will pray truly. And if you pray truly, you are a theologian."**
**Evagrios of Pontus**

Integrating your study with your spirituality can run into a huge danger. We read so much with an academic frame of mind -- studying for tests, for papers, for intellectual advancement, to impress our neighbors -- that it becomes very easy to lose an emphasis on God in all of this.

It becomes dry and instead of leading us to wisdom, we get puffed up and burnt out.

I'd like to say there's a great trick or technique or something to help avoid that. Maybe there is, but I haven't learned what it might be and suspect it's not the same for everyone.

All I can say is what I have learned from the quote I posted above. If you think you are a minister or a theologian because you know a lot... you're wrong. It's not the education or the credentials that matters. The education is only a part of learning more and more about God and his ways in this world.

Over the course of your studies you will read in depth the writings of men and women who were, who are, mature in their faith and ran a good race. But just reading their thoughts isn't enough.

They were mature because they integrated their knowledge and practice with their devotion to God.

**"If you are a theologian, you will pray truly. And if you pray truly, you are a theologian."**
**~Evagrios of Pontus**

It's not very easy to integrate our study with our spiritual life. But, find a way. Find a way of making everything you study a gift from God that helps you find your way closer to him. Lift up your studies in prayer and bathe your research in prayer and seek God's wisdom even in texts you disagree with (because the Spirit can give very interesting enlightenment about precisely why you should disagree with it).

Academics can be a form of devotions, if you let your study also be part of your life of prayer. This does take practice though, and intentional discipline. But so does prayer in general, I think.

**"If you are a theologian, you will pray truly. And if you pray truly, you are a theologian."**

# Writing as an Art and a Craft

Writing is an art and writing is a craft. What do I mean by that? Writing is an art because it is the expression of the person doing it, conveying thoughts, emotions, priorities, skills, assumptions, and everything else that goes into being human. Sure it might take a thousand words to equal just one picture, but oh what you can do in that thousand words that a picture could not do.

Say you have a picture of you and a friend camping near the Grand Canyon. Now, words cannot, I'll be the first to admit, convey the grandeur that is the Grand Canyon. Our language is useful but there are degrees of beauty (and of horror) which words simply can't keep up with. Words have their limits.

On the other hand, the picture of you and your friend all bundled up on a crisp morning, sitting before the camp stove waiting for that first cup of welcomed coffee, with the scenery of majestic crevices in the background might convey the beauty but it won't tell you about the bear that came sniffing around your tent in the night (that's why you look so tired), nor will it tell you about the odd, but nice, man with his donkey who you met on the trail the day before. We can look at that picture but we can't read your thoughts or know what you said when you first woke up, or how you're now worried about taking pictures because you forgot an extra battery.

Writing fills in all sorts of gaps and brings the reader into your thoughts and experiences. Of course this is true for telling some kind of fascinating travel story. It's even more obvious when it comes to fiction, in which the whole plot, all the characters, every disaster and every triumph all start in the mind of the writer. But, what does this have to do with writing a book review or a research essay? That's work, not art, right? Because it's boring and it's assigned and there's just not that much space for individuality to be expressed. Right?

If that's what you think, you're wrong. Entirely wrong.

Well, maybe not *entirely* wrong. Because chances are that if you think this way, you have plenty of examples. Writing often is taught to be very boring and non-expressive by people who may know a lot of rules but don't have a lot of love for the task. Sometimes these people find jobs as English or history teachers in high schools, and often make an appearance in higher levels of education. They are doing a job, not expressing an art, and they convey this attitude to their students, who surprisingly then don't find writing or reading all that interesting.

Don't let these sorts of people convince you. Because if you do, you'll be losing out on a great art, one that most everyone can pursue to one degree or another. The fact is that everything you write can, and I think should, be an expression of your creative passion. Sure, some genres like research essays insist on specific guidelines, but within even a strict framework is the opportunity to say something creative, from your heart, in a way that only you can say it. Your particularly artistic expression in a work of writing is called your "voice." Find it. But it may take time. Why?

Because writing is also a craft. It's something that you work at in order to get better. Even the best writers have to work at it, and they became the best because they worked at it. The analogy I've used for a while is that writing is a lot like running. If you run every day, you'll find you run farther and feel better while doing it. If you don't run, you think that running even the slightest distance is exhausting. The more you run, the more you can run.

The more you write, the more you can write in a given amount of time or energy. When I was in high school I was overwhelmed by the task of writing a ten page paper. Now, the same amount of pressure comes when I think about writing a book. The more I have written, the more I feel comfortable writing.

Writing isn't exactly the same as running, however. It's not just about doing it—because really bad writers may also write a lot—but also about learning how to say what you want to say in the best way possible. This takes learning from masters and it also takes a lot of trial and error. That's why I'm telling you this now. If you take the lessons from what follows in this course, and in your readings, you will be much more attuned to the craft of writing. Rather than just pumping out one paper after another, you'll learn from the challenges and by the end you will be a better writer.

Okay, we've talked a bit about seminary education in general and issues with writing.

Now I want to focus a bit more specifically on Fuller Seminary itself, as it might help your own processing along the way to understand what Fuller is about and how it goes about its mission. If you're reading this and attending a seminary other than Fuller, I encourage you to look you're your school's history and development. Doing so really helps understand your own experiences and helps you understand how you are contributing to a larger mission.

What follows is not an official statement of Fuller Seminary, just my own impressions after studying the history of this institution, spending a fair bit of time around here in two different stages of education.

---

First off, do you know the history of Fuller Seminary? If you don't, you're missing out on a big piece of why Fuller is the way it is and why it does what it does.

Here's a far too short version.

In the late 40s a number of Fundamentalist scholars, pastors, evangelists realized that the conservative Christianity which they were committed to had become fairly anti-intellectual. It wasn't always thus. Fundamentalism itself started as a way of coming to terms with what beliefs really mattered to the Christian faith, with a number of scholars (especially some from Princeton), putting together a four volume set of books called The Fundamentals. In the early 20th century battles between conservative and liberal theologies, these Fundamentals were a rallying force for many academics, institutions and denominations. Lots of Bible training schools sprang up, such as the Bible Institute of Los Angeles (BIOLA). But, by the 40s, the intellectual engagement had waned, while an anti-intellectual climate became stronger coupled with a tendency to retreat away from public life into self-contained Christian bubbles.

Well, those folks I mentioned at the start, in the 40s, saw a need for a bit of a reformation in Fundamentalism, one that would re-assert the values of learning and interaction with the broader public conversation. It would be a movement that engaged society, not one that retreated from it. This new movement was given the name Neo-Evangelicalism. Neo, because it was new, and Evangelicalism because it was a new expression of a once more common expression of Christianity that valued both academic training and evangelistic outreach.

A new movement required new expressions for training and conversation. Christianity Today was started in order to be the popular journal of the movement. And Fuller Seminary was started in order to train new ministers and Christian leaders.

That's enough history for now, but if you want to learn more have a go at *Reforming Fundamentalism* by George Marsden.

So where was I? Ah, so that's how Fuller started. It started as the flagship institution for Evangelicalism, pushing the bounds of the movement forward.

In a way it still plays this role, consistently attuned to its mission while often frustrating those on the more conservative edges of

Evangelicalism. There are a lot of argument and battles over key issues through the years. But if you understand how this history shapes and guides Fuller's continued mission, you'll understand what it is your professors are up to in your classes.

*Here's my brief, and unofficial, guide to Fuller Seminary education.*

First of all, Fuller is not a denominational school, so does not commit itself to a single denominational set of beliefs or rules or approaches. It is broadly Evangelical, meaning you'll have a lot of different people from different backgrounds and often different countries. This mixture of beliefs and approaches is very intentional.

Second, while there is a mixture, Fuller is still (like I keep saying) broadly Evangelical. It subscribes to the key elements that helped orient Evangelicalism in the beginning and continue to guide the movement today. What are these elements? A very strong commitment to Scripture, a very strong commitment to spreading the Gospel, a very strong commitment to engaging broader society, a very strong commitment to learning and training.

Third (and this may be the most important one to your studies), unlike many other institutions the goal of teaching at Fuller is not to get you to agree and argue specific points of doctrine. While you will be taught a lot of content at Fuller, there is virtually never a point at which you have to toe the line on a specific issue. While this may at first seem quite lovely, it can become very frustrating, as you will not be told what to believe, leaving you to your own discovery of wisdom about a lot of key issues.

Being told what to believe is very comforting and relaxing,

because if we know what we have to confess, then we get to know all the right statement and all the right arguments and all the right responses, leaving angst behind us. One of the reasons for the faith crises I mentioned before is because very often you'll be exposed to new directions and options, and have to determine for yourself which is the most faithful to the Gospel.

Why does Fuller let you figure out these things on your own? Because at the core of Fuller Seminary is the intent to teach you how to think, not what to think. The teachers here want you to learn how to learn, they want you to learn how to gain more information, get into the sources, getting used to the process of self-teaching, so that once you go from her e, your learning is only beginning.

This encourages a creative exploration, that allows students to argue their positions and come to terms with key issues on their own. The goal at Fuller is to provide you with basic content to be sure, but even more so to provide you with the introduction to using the tools that will help you gather more and more content.

For the most part, you can argue back against professors if you feel you have a point to make. And if you can prove your points all the better! It makes for lively conversation. Professors will often push back, but in a way that hones your skills and exposes your weaknesses, something which sharpens your skills. But sometimes you will be right, and the better you know your tools the better you'll be able to make your case.

For instance, in a previous class, I corrected an aspect of one student's bibliography. He pushed back, showing where his citation was right and my correction was wrong. Which is excellent work! At this stage of learning you're not expected to merely parrot back information, but are becoming capable to engage the core tools on your own. The key, as with the student I mentioned, was that he used the tools provided not his own opinions. Learn the tools and you can use them to support your work and ideas.

Again, Fuller seminary will teach you a lot of content, and there will be tests on this content, and there will be lots of stuff that you will simply have to learn. But this isn't about you merely absorbing more and more. Learning all that content provides a foundation for more learning and gives you more insight on how to learn. The key isn't so often the learning the facts (which might be forgotten after a test) but learning how to use the tools so that in any given setting you can learn what is required so that you can teach those in your congregations, in your ministries, in whatever setting.

# Motivation and Writing

I mentioned before that one of the best ways to improve as a writer is by writing a lot. But how do you get to writing a lot? Indeed, the most difficult challenge to the task of writing isn't related to grammar or research or organization. The most difficult challenge to writing, and writing a lot, is motivation. Those who write the most are driven to work at it for some reason or another. Which means that if you can find the motivation you will have a much better chance to write a well-constructed paper.

In any kind of school setting, however, you're not only dealing with your motivation, or lack thereof. You're also dealing with the teacher's motivation. These two motivations are generally always quite different. And, honestly, it is very difficult to care too much about any motivation that is not your own.

For the most part, the teacher's motivation for assigning book reviews or research essays or anything else is not so they can learn something new from your writing. They are not looking for some brilliant new insight or awakening, nor are they looking to be put on the right track in their own field of study.

In higher education, the teacher has often spent as much, or more, time studying this particular subject than you have been alive. And even if this is not the case for older students or younger teachers, it's still the case that for them to be in the position they are in, teachers have dedicated an immense amount of time and effort to master the field they are now teaching.

They don't begin each new term looking forward to all the new material the students will teach them. The best teachers, to be sure, do learn from their students, and one of the best ways to master any subject is to teach it. But this is not why assignments are given, even if it is occasionally a byproduct.

The motivation for a teacher in assigning a research essay, book review, or other writing task is to see if you, in fact, can write one of these assignments following the proper guidelines. In other words, teachers are generally more interested in the technical aspects of an assignment than in what you, personally, think about the topic. They want to know that you have the ability to organize your thoughts, write coherent sentences, document your sources in the proper fashion, and otherwise conform to the standards that have been established in that particular field for that particular kind of writing.

A student properly formatting a footnote is something that gives a teacher joy. Yeah, it's not a particularly exciting sort of joy, but teachers will take what they can get, and what they often get are papers that are a mess in terms of formatting or structure.

I remember when I would get papers returned in college and seminary. I often had "good intro" or words to that effect written after my introduction. I thought it was an odd comment to get regularly until I got to the point I was grading papers. Good introductions are rare creatures indeed! And I make the same sorts of comments on student papers because I want to make note when I have a sighting of such an endangered species.

What a teacher wants is not that difficult. Usually they will even give you some detailed instructions about what exactly they are looking for. For the most part these instructions are pretty easy, as long as you understand the concepts. But because most students don't see the assignment from the perspective of the teacher they make the paper much more difficult than it should be, and often don't even get to the easy parts the teacher wants. This is because students tend to get caught up in their own motivation, or lack of it.

What is the student's motivation? Because writing is, in essence, an art, any time we sit down to write we are expressing a part of our self, whether we intend to or not. If we are intentional about it, we find writing to be more satisfying. If we are not, writing can become jumbled and confusing and frustrating because there is this drive to express our self mixed in with all sorts of other, supposed, goals like getting a good grade, or just getting it done, or impressing the teacher with your brilliance, or some other reason which doesn't quite carry enough push to bring real motivation.

So, it helps to know what really motivates the writer, and how to make this work for your rather than against you. Ultimately, what motivates a writer is curiosity. The most motivated writers are writing about something they are interested in and want to learn more about. The process of writing becomes a process of exploration, putting vague thoughts into a coherent expression and putting dispersed research into a nicely ordered package.

A writer is motivated when he or she understands this whole process as helping find a way to new insights or answers. The student is motivated by what is interesting or helpful to their learning. The professor is motivated by determining if the students understand the basics of the process. These are two entirely different motivations, though they need not be contrary to each other.

The best papers are those that fulfill the motivation of the student in being personally interesting while also fulfilling the expectations of the teacher in following all the right guidelines. The worst are the papers in which the student is uninterested and makes all sorts of mistakes that the teacher has to penalize. Teachers want to read good writing and good students want to learn. Teachers do not want to give bad grades and students do not want to be bored.

If you get this in your head, you will try to understand, and maybe find, your own motivation while keeping in mind the teacher's motivation. If you do that you will write a significantly better and more interesting paper. And it's not that hard. Students make it much, much harder than it should be, adding frustration on top of bother, then getting a bad grade as a result.

Each time you have to write, whatever it is you have to write, **ask yourself two questions:**

First, **what is your motivation**? If you can't answer it right away, find an answer quickly. Find some way of making the assignment interesting to you. Maybe you are answering a question you've had for a while. Or maybe it is trying to come to terms with arguments you disagree with, so that you can better understand them and critique them. Or using a review or research essay to give you notes for continued study later on. There are lots of ways of making the assignment personally useful to your own goals and interests. Find it, and you'll be much more motivated to write.

Second, **what is your teacher's motivation**? If you can't answer that right away, you almost certainly can find the answer in how the teacher assigned it. What are they looking for? What are the guidelines and rules they have given? Is there a grading rubric that tells you exactly how they will be grading? Read the syllabus or any related handouts, and the answer is almost certainly there. If it's not given to you, or you can't find it, ask.

The teacher will almost certainly tell you what will motivate them to give a good grade. There will probably be a list, and it might even be numbered or bulleted. Follow it, and you will motivate the teacher to give you a good grade.

It is more difficult for the writer to find motivation. Especially when you are not choosing the assignment or even the topic. It is hard to get excited about something that you did not choose and that you have to do. But, and this is key, if you don't see something interesting in the assignment right away, keep looking until you find it. Find something to motivate you in everything you write and you will write better, write more fluidly, be more interesting, and begin to take shape as a good writer.

Good writers are not merely people who have mastered good grammar or the right way to footnote a specific source. Good writers are people who find something interesting to write about no matter the topic or situation, because they look for what is interesting. The more you look for it, the more you will get into the habit of noticing and discovering that which makes you curious.

Like I said before, writing is an art and writing is a craft. Students are most interested in writing as art while teachers are most interested in writing as a craft. This distinction gives no end of trouble because students are often baffled when a teacher doesn't reward them for some brilliant idea or expression of new insight. Meanwhile the teachers are often baffled about how many of their students entirely ignored the requirements given for the assignment, often making up their own priorities, formatting, and just about everything else.

Now for a note on **sources for a research paper**:

**I. Use a primary source for each person you are involving in your argument**. For instance, if you say Barth said, "Something Brilliant," and then go on to fill out what else Barth said or use Barth as a part of your argument, then go and read Barth, at least a little bit. Never entirely trust another person's perspective on what someone believes. Always go to, at least a little bit, to that someone.

Learning how to go directly to the primary sources is a huge part of studying at this level of education. In high school or undergraduate work you can get way with depending on the opinions of others. Now, there is no excuse for that, and given the easy accessibility of writings online, there is no reason not to read the primary sources.

And another connected though. Oftentimes, the primary source, the original thinker, is much more interesting and inspirational than the people writing about him or her. Get over being intimidated by primary sources and make them your first goal for study.

For those of you studying church history a great resource for church history writings is the Christian Classics Ethereal Library (www.ccel.org) or other online collections

**II. Use enough secondary sources that you have a fair balance of perspectives on the topic at hand**. It is best to have at least one that is sympathetic to your topic/position and one that is critical. That way you are viewing and describing the issue fairly.

**III. Tertiary sources are good to get guidance on where else to go**, but for research papers you probably don't want to depend on these, except to fill out some definitions or add other types of filler.

The goal is to get a sense of the conversation on the topic you're discussing, so that you know what was said originally and you know how others might interpret it. The key is that you should use a source if you have a question you want to confirm or want to support an assertion you're making. How many? As many sources as it takes to have a solid foundation of each element.

A more direct answer to the question "How many sources do I need?" might be something like: I'd be careful using anything less than 5 sources and you're probably okay with a ten page research paper having between 6-10, though I certainly don't penalize for having too many.

**Formatting:**
For just about every paper at Fuller, you need to **use 12pt Times New Roman font and 1 inch margins**. Note that some versions of Word have the original default of 1.5 inch margins, so be careful with that. Footnotes should be 10pt font and single spaced. If you have a quote that is more than 3 lines long, you need to start the quote on a new line, indent it, and make it single spaced. Always format your paper exactly as specified. It is good practice in paying attention to details and it is another factor in helping the grader give you a good grade.

# Faith Crises in Seminary

Almost everyone who enters or hears about seminary and will encounter the topic of faith crisis. It's an important topic and so I wanted to devote some time to discussing it more fully.

Here's what it boils down to.

You **will** have a crisis of faith of one kind or another while in Seminary. You may even have several kinds or possibly one of every possible kind.

As one great guide puts it: **Don't Panic**.

Now, I know, you may be thinking, "I've a sure faith on a solid foundation. Bring it on!" Good. I'm glad you feel strong in your faith at the beginning. However, if that's your attitude then your crisis of faith will come from a direction you least expect it. And it's hard to tell where we might least expect it, since the very nature of least expectations, it's not something that comes to mind.

Different kinds of crises of faith arise for different reasons. Here's a few that come to mind:

1. **A Crisis of Faith due to critical reading of Scripture or theology.** You will probably be exposed to much broader ways of coming to terms with Scripture, either as a whole or in parts, and specific theological issues than you ever have before. Indeed, Scripture is the sort of thing that if we approach it on its own terms it challenges us in all kinds of ways. In most of life we can ignore those challenges either by retreating into settled dogmatic positions or by putting the questions off to the side. You can't do that as much in

Seminary because professors will intentionally force you to confront various challenges. By the way, in Seminary "critical" doesn't mean criticizing. A critical reading is one that looks to address a topic with an open perspective and honest response, which may or may not offer significant challenges to the topic at hand. You can heartily affirm something, but still approach it critically by addressing both the positive and negative aspects. But far too often we have a binary kind of learning, yes or no, good or bad, wrong or right. You have to learn how to engage something critically, so you can understand the problems that might be there while affirming that which is useful or good in it.

2. **A crisis of faith by becoming too idealistic.** You will read all kinds of great stuff. You will read some great theology. You will read the masters of ministry. Life doesn't always, or even often, match up with the possibilities that a seminary education suggests. So, when your experiences slam into your studies, you're going to be tempted to dispute one or the other, and often this involves becoming quite mad at either your experiences or your studies. It's not that either are wrong, it's just that part of your continuing role is learning how to integrate these two sides of your learning.

3. ... (meaning a lot of other stuff might do it).

**Here's some thoughts that may not help avert the crisis, but might be worthwhile reminders to help you through it.**

**1.** Your professors know a whole lot more about the subjects than you do. They know all the problems and frustrations and critical challenges on any given topic, whether it be ministry, theology, Scripture, church history. And to a person at Fuller Seminary, your professors will be extremely faithful followers of Christ. So, if you come to something that you can't see past or which undermines some assumption, know there are men and women who have encountered that same challenge, and have found their way through it, often with a deepened, not lessened, faith.

**2.** A crisis of faith comes from having faith in something that cannot sustain it. We often say our faith is in Christ, but oftentimes we have a faith that isn't quite as pure. We need something else to help us with our belief, and it is likely something that can and is challenged.

It is important for us to reorient our faith onto a sustainable source, God himself, because we will be required to encounter the crises of faith of others. Even if we temporarily solve or resolve our own crisis -- say with a stance on Scripture or something -- unless we have a firm universal foundation we have nothing to offer those with different crises.

**3.** This is where real faith comes into play. Sometimes everything seems to have crumbled away. Sometimes we are intellectually or emotionally exhausted. Don't stop there. Don't stop in the wilderness. God calls his people to keep moving forward even when they don't see what is ahead, especially when they don't see what is ahead. I guarantee you that if you press on in seeking God during seasons of challenge or silence or confusion or disbelief, you will find resolution at some point. And by walking through that wilderness, by slogging forward, you will be a much better thinker and minister. The wilderness makes us honest and exposes our weaknesses.

# How to Read in Seminary

At this level of study there's required reading and there's reading that's required. In other words, there's reading that is assigned in the syllabus and on top of this there is the reading required for research papers or other such assignments. Which means that you have a whole lot of reading to do in general.

One of the skills to learn in graduate studies is how to effectively and efficiently study a book in the shortest amount of time possible. Now, I'm tentative about sharing this information, because I really do want you to read the required reading closely. Those books were chosen out of a myriad of different options because they have all kinds of very helpful guidance to serve as a foundation.

So, if you promise to continue to read the required reading thoroughly, I'll move on. If not... well, close this page now.

First of all, other some intro courses have required a book titled *How to Read a Book*. I didn't require it for my intro to seminary class, as I wanted students to instead read books that were content related to seminary studies. Also, I've never read it. But a lot of people recommend it, so if you're struggling to get a handle on the reading requirements, it might be a great resource for you. Instead of learning through trial and error, and taking years, this might be a quick way to train you to use better reading habits.

What follows is what I've learned over the years in various places.

First off, get an overview of the book. Read the back cover, or dust jacket, or wherever there's a short blurb about the book and the author. Get to know who and what you're dealing with. Open it up, look at the Table of Contents. See where the book is headed and what it covers.

Second, and related to the first, read a short selection. Some people like to read the first paragraph and the last. I personally hate reading the end first, probably for the same reason I hate it when anyone tells me about the plot of a movie or the to watch previews of "next week's show" or to hear any of the other details that get in the way of a fresh experience of a plot. I like the build up and the resolution to come as a surprise.

So, I tend to open the book at random, read a paragraph or two. This gives me a sense of the writer's style, difficulty, approach, etc. That way I know what to expect in terms of commitment. Is this going to be an easy book that I can breeze through? Or is it a book that is going to require significant mental energy and I need to use my most focused times of day for it?

That latter point is a big consideration, and one that if you don't know, you should learn. Everyone has different times of day in which they are most focused and aware. For me it's in the morning. I write and read significantly faster and with more focus before noon. After noon and in the evening, my brain just slows down. So, as much as possible, I try to do the bulk of my reading and writing in the morning.

Third, find a way of taking notes while you read. Reading a book already takes a lot of time, reading it again to find good quotes or main points adds a lot to the frustration. Again, everyone has a different method.

I use one of those four color bic pens and a six inch ruler. I don't have a rigid rule for how I use each color, though black is usually some kind of main point or the beginning of a section, while red is usually a good quote.

Why four colors? Because if you're underlining or highlighting a lot, a page gets filled up and if everything looks the same, then it all blends together again, so nothing sticks out. The key is to make sure that what you're marking up sticks out to you as you quickly review the book later.

I can open just about any book I've read and within moments tell you the basic outline, the main point, key quotes, and such, even if I haven't read the book in years.

Why the ruler? Because it helps everything look neat.

I also make marks like little checks or stars in the margins for really key sections, and I write words there as well to describe the topic being discussed, or if the author has written their thesis or goal or some other major aspect to understand their project.

Which means my books tend to get messy with markings, but are extremely useful to me because of it. It's almost to the point that if I don't have a four color pen with me, it's a waste of my time to read a book, as I'd have to read it again later anyhow.

Whatever works for you, find a way of taking notes or making marks that helps you quickly find key information after you're finished reading.

Now to the reading itself (and here's the part that makes me nervous about sharing) Writers tend to organize their material in standard ways. Part of this course is about teaching you to conform your writing in a way that fits the academic standard and part of the nice thing about having that standard it that most books become a lot easier to read more quickly.

So fifth, always read the introduction or first chapter (if that's serving as the introduction). Here you'll find all kinds of helpful guidance like what the author is going to say, how he or she is going to go about arguing their case, and most importantly you'll usually get the main point of the book. Getting to know their main argument at the beginning saves a lot of time.

Sixth, if you know you're going to only have time to skim the book, then read the conclusion. It will sum up what the author has done, how they've proven their case, and the main goal of the book.

If you do just these, you can often have a sense of the whole book in just a short amount of time. But that leaves out a lot of details, and sometimes those details are very important, especially with history or Scripture studies.

Seventh, if you have more time to spend with the book, but not time to read it closely word for word, you can prioritize what you read depending on how much time you have. In a way, with each smaller section, the advice stays the same. Read the beginning and read the end.

Read the first and last paragraph of a chapter.

Read the first and last sentence of a paragraph.

This won't get you everything, but if you do just this, you'll get most of what you need to know from a book. If you don't have time to do this, then follow the great counsel: the last shall be first.

Read the last sentences of a paragraph and the last paragraph of a chapter.

Eighth, take breaks. Depending on how used you are to reading and how difficult the material is, your brain can handle only so much in a single sitting. You may force yourself to sit and read through the entire assignment in one sitting, but after even a short while, you'll find your mind drifting, and while you're technically reading you're not absorbing anything.

Which means that even if you have spent 2 straight hours reading, only the first 1/2 hour was actually of any use. So it feels like you're spending a lot of time, and learning very little.

I've found that my brain can handle about 20 pages of theology reading at a time. I read about 20 pages, I take a small break, like 5 or 10 minutes. When I start again, I'm reading with a lot more focus and reading faster. So even though I take breaks, I get much more reading done.

I also find that about 100 pages is my normal limit for a day. If I read 100 pages, I feel good about my efforts and even if I have more reading to do, I feel like I've made good use of my day. Because after that, my brain gets mushy and I'm not making connections anymore with the reading.

Each person is different, and so it's important to learn what is the best time and what is the best duration of reading that helps you get the most out of your effort.

And those are my tips on reading.

# Choosing and Prioritizing Sources

So, since I've already talked about motivation for reading, how to read, and how many sources to have for a research paper, it's a good time to talk about the kinds of sources and how to prioritize what you find.

Here's a basic guide.

**The more academic, the better.** Something from a peer-reviewed journal, or an academic book, or written by a scholar on the subject is a very high quality source (even if you disagree with their conclusions or method).

**The newer, the better.** This is a tricky one, because it's not always technically true, but is a good enough rule in general. One downside is that if it is too new, it hasn't had time to be considered itself. But the rule is still worth considering. Why? Scholarly knowledge changes over time and generally becomes better, as previous theories are considered and reviewed, either becoming useful or discarded. Plus, newer works often have more up to date footnotes, from which you can find other helpful and relevant sources.

This factor is especially true with volumes like Bible dictionaries, other reference works, commentaries. Information gets outdated pretty quickly. While a lot of popular Bible and Theology studies are revered for being classics, and are often free or cheap, so are used a lot in churches or popular approaches to studying, they're often not at all suitable for academic research, because they're just too out of date with a lot of their information.

For discussions on positions taken by a tradition or denomination or other established group, **the more official the better**. For instance, if you want to say what Catholics believe then you pretty much have to refer to Vatican II, which is the core set of documents defining the church in our era. Other denominations and organizations have their own sets of documents.

A related priority has to do with the contributions of individuals. **The closer the source to the subject at hand, the better.** If you say a theologian believes something, quote that theologian or cite where they say they believe that which you say they believe.

In other words, don't let a secondary source put words into the mouth of an organization or another person. Secondary sources are often very helpful, but they can also have their own agenda or simply misinterpret what they're studying.

If you can't cite the specific person or specific organization itself, for some reason, the next best is to **trust someone who knows them best**. For instance, a faithful educated Catholic is more trustworthy on Catholic doctrine than an anti-Roman Catholic Baptist. That's not to say an anti-Roman Catholic Baptist is wrong on all their critiques, just that if you are being fair to all sides, get a sympathetic perspective by someone who knows and often is committed to that side.

Another example: Say you want to know more about Wolfhart Pannenberg. There is a lot written about him, as he's a very established and influential theologian. Stanley Grenz was his student, however, and so the books by Grenz on Pannenberg are especially trustworthy.

**Experts in the field are better.** Scholars who have established themselves and are known as being trustworthy by other scholars are better resources than someone no one else quotes or knows.

Some of the factors of choosing best resources come over time and experience. You get to know the key experts in a field and you get a feel for what is scholarly and useful. Research becomes more instinctual and you know a good source when you see it, and know how to find the better sources quickly.

# Writing an introduction paragraph

In the intro to seminary class I used to teach, I had students write an introduction paragraph in the third week of class. It's an awkward but helpful exercise. Awkward, because their research paper was not due until the end of the quarter, so they likely had not yet started research for it. It was helpful because it pushed students to think more about writing their paper earlier, rather than the night before it's due.

But that's a minor reason. The larger reason is that by having students work on writing an introduction paragraph early, it helps students think about their research project in more approachable chunks. These kinds of projects can be extremely daunting if we think about them as a single task. Breaking the project into more approachable tasks makes it seem much more doable.

And breaking the project down into particular kinds of tasks, helps students build your project upon each piece. By working on a project in a certain order, students are building a framework that helps them fill in the blank spaces and points you to what you need to do and where you need to go.

Starting with an outline is often good. Now, you very rarely need to turn in an outline, and whether you write one at all is likely up to you. But, it is useful as a beginning framework, as a way of you thinking about this project and a way for others to learn how you are thinking about it.

Most professors and TAs are more than willing to talk about projects, so make use of them in that way and you'll find your papers being much sharper.

Now, while the outline serves as a diagram of sorts, plans for what should be done, the introductory paragraph is the first actual building you do. To keep up with the building metaphor, the introductory paragraph helps clear the ground and serves as the foundation of what you'll build next.

If you have a shaky foundation, you'll have a shaky construction.

In a way, an introductory paragraph serves as a companion of your outline. It is taking your outline and putting it into sentences, along with some inner motivation and goals that steer how you will write.

Now that this preliminary discussion is out of the way, let's get into the introductory paragraph itself.

Memorize these three words: **Purpose**, **Plan**, **Thesis**.

Your introduction needs to have these three elements in it. If you have these three elements in it, that means you have these three elements in your mind, and that means your paper will have a cohesive direction.

Here's what I mean by these elements:

**Purpose:** Why are you writing this paper? Now, this is a bit tricky because it can wander all kinds of directions. So keep in mind a couple of important questions. **What are you writing about? Why is writing about this topic important?** This part of the introduction introduces the reader to your topic and fills in a little bit why you think it is worthwhile for you to address this topic. Now, there can be all kinds of reasons for why you think it is important, but share what seems the most vital.

Another way of looking at this section is going back to the assignment a couple of weeks ago in which I had you write about your topic.

In that assignment, I wanted your topic and also why you chose it. That's basically your purpose. Ah, now you're seeing that I do have something in mind with those assignments.

This purpose can be expressed creatively or it can be direct. I generally like to begin with a bit of a creative introduction, both to charge up my own thoughts and also to set the tone for the reading in general. I tell a story or give an image or otherwise put the paper into a context in which I show why I think the topic is important. If you're a creative writer, this helps the paper feel more creative from the start. But, don't get distracted. The introduction should be no more than a page long, and ideally should be about a 1/2 page for a ten page paper.

**Plan**: This is your outline, put into sentences. Pretty straightforward. Tell the reader how you will go about writing your paper. You don't have to be extremely detailed, but do discuss the elements that were in the basic outline I described. Say what you will do first, second, third, and fill in necessary details about what such tasks will do.

For instance, if you're saying first you "will write about Baptism in the Catholic Church", add what aspects you will focus on. For instance: "In the first section I will discuss baptism in the Catholic Church, looking at the key theology as expressed in Vatican II, then looking at the practices that arise from this theology."

So, again the plan is telling the reader your outline and approach.

**Thesis**: This is the big one. The one that confuses most students and the one that is left out of most papers, even after saying it is required. So **pay attention** to what comes next. Of course, if you're not paying attention you probably missed that encouragement to *pay attention*, but it makes me feel better that I've done my part in getting you to **pay attention**.

Your thesis, put simply, is what you are going to argue. It is what you are trying to convince the reader to agree with or understand. It is, basically, the **goal of your paper put into a sentence**.

Now, remember the first weeks of class I had you fill in the blanks, **The Old Testament is _____ to me**, and assignments like that? That was thesis writing training. I had you then fill out in a few sections why you said that, giving you a framework and plan. That one sentence was your thesis. Now, there might be a number of ways to approach a topic, or get at a doctrine, or approach the issues at hand. In your thesis, you are telling the reader what you, specifically, are going to argue.

Personally, I have always liked to build up the tension, creating a plot of sorts that then hits the reader with my conclusion. But that's wrong. Don't build up any tension. Don't hold anything back for a grand finale. In a research paper thesis you are giving away your ending right at the beginning. You are saying, "this is what I am going to prove."

Now, some papers will have a much more clear kind of thesis than others. However, just about every paper has a thesis of one kind or another, because you as the writer have some particular goal in mind as you're writing. There's something that is steering you to write the way you are writing, and that something is generally your thesis, it's the driving conclusion that you're going to spend a lot of time trying to establish.

Now, more than just giving away your ending at the beginning, thus taking away any suspense, the thesis serves as a guiding beacon for what you focus on. **Everything in your paper should move the argument towards your thesis.** There might be a lot of other interesting elements in your topic, but they are extraneous if they don't help your paper progress towards your thesis.

That means having your thesis at the beginning is a great help to your reader, so they know what you are trying to do, and a help to you so that you keep your focus where it needs to be.

So, what are the three words you need to keep in mind, both for your introduction and for the whole project?

**Purpose, plan, thesis.**

# Thoughts on studying theology

In 2013, I finished a PhD in theology at Fuller, so I've spent quite a bit of time studying and thinking about theological topics and the discipline of theology and thinking about thinking about studying theology. Yes, I likely think too much, but now that is part of my job.

The interesting part, to me at least, is that if someone had told me while I was doing my undergraduate work that I would eventually go on to do a PhD in systematic theology, I wouldn't even have laughed, because the thought would have been too absurd. Theology, after all, was that way in which people interfered in the clear teaching of the Bible, adding all sorts of extra bits and pieces, distracting everyone from what we should be thinking about. Which of course is God, salvation, evangelism, the church, and becoming better Christians.

I was much more into the study of history back then, and loved reading the thoughts of those great Christians who came before us, who had risked their lives and livelihoods, who had pondered deeply the works of God and sought him with all their life. I loved reading about their struggles coming to terms with who God was and what God was doing in their lives and in their communities.

When I started at Fuller, I took a systematic theology class during my first quarter, to get it out of the way. I ended up doing really well in it. Indeed, I ended up really enjoying the reading. Turns out all those things I was interested in reading about, all those things I was interested in focusing on in my own life, were basically what the study of theology is all about.

Who knew? I thought it was obscure philosophy and big words and complicated concepts, making more difficult what was otherwise pretty clear.

As I wrestled with my own problems in life and tried to come to terms with the suffering others were experiencing, and trying to make sense of what it means to live a Christian life in this world, trying to come to terms with the fact that even though I was saved I didn't really seem to be experiencing the presence of Christ... well I was encountering the subjects of theology.

When I was working in a church and seeing how lots of people around me were really good at different tasks and how there was a wholeness and joy during times of really deep community connection, I was encountering theology there too.

Theology is all around us, after all, and it's a mistake to relegate it to the back rooms of philosophical esoterica. Everyone is a theologian, because we all go beyond merely existing and think about life's meaning and purpose and how it all fits together. We all have thoughts about God and his work (indeed whether using 'his' is appropriate).

We wake up each morning facing a day filled with mystery and our mind tries to organize the events and the habits and the goals into some kind of coherent system, one that helps us make sense of ourselves and the world around us.

That's theology. While we're all theologians in this respect, the question is whether we're good theologians. And the answer to that is generally, 'No, we're not." We focus on some areas, but don't reflect on how those areas impact or intersect with others. We make sure one small portion of our encounter with God is orderly and sensible, but try to ignore a lot of other areas, which may be too difficult or dark.

We contain ourselves within established packages we call theological traditions, maintaining foes with those who dispute doctrines that we ourselves have trouble describing. We feel safe in a small enclosed room.

But God is calling us to more. And part of this more is taking the risk in getting to know him, in seeking out the fullness of his revelation and calling and kingdom.

That's what theology is about. Or at least what I think it should be about.

The word theology basically just means "words concerning God'. It's the study of God, and that's a pretty big, expansive study I think.

Some in previous centuries tried to really manage what such a study should look like, and like any field they organized themselves and gave standards and formats that fit into the guild of those who professionally studied God. That's changing, as now theology can look like many things and approach the study of God from many directions, all trying to contribute wisdom but knowing that no one could ever really understand the whole reality of God.

This whole revelation, this whole reality, is the textbook from which we gather insight. That's why this study wasn't the one we started with.

We started from Scripture because that is the testimony of God's revelation in key moments throughout history, declaring his works and his message through divinely validated spokespeople.

Indeed, we say one of those messengers didn't just speak for God, he was God, though as his words were passed through the words of others, we always have a mediator, giving us the witness that we can't experience ourselves.

Is it a truthful testimony throughout? That's a key question in theology, and if it is truthful, then there are all kinds of various priorities that must be balanced to find a cohesive, coherent teaching.

That is something we wrestle with today and something that followers of God have wrestled with throughout history. So, from the Bible we study church history, learning how men and women throughout the centuries have understood those core teachings as well as the continuing work of God in their eras and lives.

Some stumbled along the way, some found great wisdom and success, most were a mixture of those, so we learn both from their contributions and from their eras how to conceive of God.

With Bible and Church history in mind we the try to come to terms with who God is, bringing also other voices and influences, which can come from the many directions that God is active. What directions are those?

Well, that's a question theology has to ask, making the task of theology a bit of a spiral, maybe sometimes just a circle. It has to figure out the method that goes into studying theology before and while it puts these assumptions into practice to consider Scripture, history and all of life as one coherent narrative.

We assert that God is himself coherent and whole, but we lack all the pieces and lack the wisdom to make the connections to how this is true. So we wrestle and we argue and we write and we ponder. All of this in trying to come to terms with what we can know, as we seek to better understand God and his broad work.

So, welcome to theology. It is about everything really, but about everything in a way that focuses on God's involvement and identity.

Quite a glorious field of study indeed.

We should, no doubt, start this study with a fair amount of prayer.

## Footnotes

Ladies and gentleman, I want to introduce you to something I think you'll learn to appreciate, become friends with even, invite over to your house for some wine maybe. Okay, maybe not that last bit. However, maybe it's even more important that that.

You know what I'm talking about because it's in the title, but you still don't believe me that this is what all the fanfare is about.

I'm just talking about footnotes, right?

Just footnotes?! I scoff at that 'just'. **A well-wielded footnote is immensely powerful and impressive.** Good footnoting is often the most apparent indicator between an expert or a newbie. It's very difficult to overestimate the importance of a good footnote.

Well, that's not true. It's actually quite easy to overestimate the importance of a good footnote. Good footnotes are the cause of world hunger. A good footnote can defeat the entire gathered Communist armies. See, I overestimated the importance of a footnote twice right there, and it was pretty easy to do.

Let me start over. **It's very difficult to overestimate the importance of a footnote in regards to academic essay writing.** There, that makes it much more specific and much more true.

So, what's the big deal with footnotes and why do I appear to be infatuated with them?

Well, let me give you some reasons.

For most people, a footnote is a citation, a way to mark that something you write is actually from something another person wrote. That's true. That's the most basic purpose of a footnote. You make a note of a source, you cite it, so that you aren't charged with plagiarism. If you quote a source, or paraphrase a source, or find specific information from a source, you have to cite it.

And, so you know, the style for formatting a footnote is different than formatting a bibliography. There are a lot more commas and parentheses, and less periods. **So, make sure you know and use the proper footnote style!**

If the only thing you can learn about footnotes is this first use, then you're good. You're not advanced. But you're in good shape. **Cite right and format right, and you'll be fine.** That's the minimum use for footnotes.

Ah, but wait, there's more! Not only can a footnote cite. **A footnote can be used for many other purposes.**

For instance, do you have a citation from one book but know another book that talks about the same issue in the same or different way. Add that citation to your footnote using the phrase "see also".

Is there a whole list of books that you read on a specific issue, but don't have time or space to interact with them all. **Share your research in a footnote!** List as many relevant books as you want. This means that more than just citation, a footnote is the place for you to show off. You let the reader know that you're attentive to your area of study and you want to show how much work you've done and what other people have said.

Sometimes, in the interest of saving space, I'll make an assertion in the main text that an author believes some point or position. Then in the footnote, I'll quote the author, adding support and depth to my assertion.

**Another big use of footnotes is as a way of discussing an issue that is relevant to but not crucial for the main text.** Your main text should be very sharply focused on the task at hand, proving your thesis. But along the way you might discover interesting related issues, or discussions between theologians, or a nifty fact, or a word study, or just about anything else. It would be diverting and distracting in the main text, so you might think you have to shove it in anyhow or to leave it out. You have a third option! You guessed it, footnote it!

**In general, a footnote provides you an amazing tool to impress your readers with your grasp of the subject at hand while staying very focused in the main text.** A footnote provides a way of showing what you know and what you think and anything else you have found.

Again, at the very minimum, you need to use footnotes to cite your sources. But, if you go beyond this, and use footnotes to your advantage, you can help your paper go to the next level of quality and interest.

So, why did I encourage you to forget about bibilographies at the top? Well, because your footnotes do all the heavy lifting of citation you often don't need to include a separate bibliography. Sometimes it is required, so check in each course, but in general a bibliography is only important as a personal resource for your research. Which means that you don't need to fret about formatting one, unless you're turning it in with an essay. Fret instead about properly formatting those footnotes.

When you're reading an academic book, don't just read the content, look at the stylistic elements as well. How did they compose their introduction? What is the framework of the book? Look at their footnotes. Look at articles and every source you use in your courses as a way of seeing how everything comes together and how they are designed. Footnotes are especially useful but using them is indeed an art.

Learn what you can do, and how to master the footnote, and you'll be that much closer to becoming a fully operational research essay writer.

Oh, and **I'll end with a very practical point.**

**The first time you cite** a source, you give full bibliographic information according to the prescribed Turabian footnote style. **Thereafter**, you give a shortened version. This is usually the author's last name then a comma then a page number. If you're using more than one source by an author, you give the author, the title of the source, and then the page number.

Look at the examples in Houghton and Houghton, in the example paper I wrote, and in other texts. See how others do it, and follow their lead.

Happy footnoting to all and to all a good cite!

# Writing a conclusion

Writing an essay isn't hardest part of a research essay. The hardest part isn't even doing all the research or reading all the research. These may be time consuming, but they aren't the hardest. Those are straightforward tasks, or they should be at least. The hardest part is coming to terms with all the research, all the various questions, all the assorted issues, and making this fit into a tight, coherent ten page essay.

It's hard because we so often approach these sorts of projects thinking only about the whole -- thinking about having to write ten pages or more in order to get a passing grade in this class. Don't think like that. And that's what I'm trying to have you do... or not do.

Instead of thinking in terms of a big ten page project, think in terms of the component sections. Think in terms of each issue and each part. That's why I had my intro to seminary students start with an outline. I wanted them to break down their project into separate sections. Then I had them write an introduction, because I wanted them to focus on a specific thesis and give clarity to their interests in the big topic.

The next week, I had them write a conclusion. Because by writing a conclusion, I hoped to give them a finish line of sorts, knowing where they need to be by the end.

An outline, with an introduction and conclusion, provides you with scaffolding to fill in, a framework for you to attach all the pieces. You won't get confused trying to figure out what to do next. You'll have the checklist in front of you. (How's that for a lot of mixed metaphors?)

In addition, writing a conclusion provides a place for you to talk about related issues that you didn't (or at least won't) cover in your essay. It gets you thinking about your specific task in light of the bigger topic. You see, most people do just the opposite, they think about the bigger topic and then lose sight of the specific task, making for a research paper that tries too much, makes too many generalizations, and otherwise is a big ol' mess.

Don't turn in a mess, that's a good rule of thumb for any assignment.

So, do I look for in a conclusion? Well, if you've written your introduction, which generally happens before writing a conclusion, then writing a conclusion is itself pretty straightforward. You remember the elements of an introduction? Let's say them out loud together: Purpose, Plan, Thesis.

Well, these are elements in a conclusion too. But not quite the same as what you wrote before. A conclusion is a review of what you've done, a tying together of various threads so that you can assert your thesis as a proven or established point. You remind us of your overall purpose, bringing us back to the big picture that may have gotten lost in the details.

You tell us what you argued and what such arguments lead us to. You note how each step points us closer to your goal, and that goal is your thesis, so you give us that thesis as a proven point, showing why it is true in light of what you have studied.

Don't stop there, however. A conclusion is also a place to say what you haven't said. Note your focus and note further areas of study related to your topic. Such areas might be significant aspects of the larger study, that you bypassed in order to focus precisely on a narrow study. Or it could be research that is provoked by your thesis, and suggests further areas you see as necessary for a better overall understanding.

Finally, you can end with a review of the significance. Why is what you wrote important in light of the topic's overall importance? What are we left with? You might also note more pastoral or missional directions such a study evokes.

As you can see, a conclusion can be a very creative exercise where you let out all the threads or passion or interests that you had to set aside along the way in order to stay focused on the topic at hand. You are free, here, to let loose with why you think this matters to you, to me, to anyone.

Want it to be even more straightforward? Look at your introduction again. Use it as a model for how to write your conclusion. Instead of saying what you will do, say what you "have" done. Rephrase it so that it sounds like you went step by step, then re-approach your thesis so that it sounds like you proved it in your paper. Tell me why this stuff matters. There's your conclusion.

To summarize what I just said, I'll give you the relevant section of the rubric. These are the things I look for in the grading essays:

> Conclusion:
> Appropriate length (about a page)
>
> Ability to pull together various ideas discussed in the paper (in light of the purpose and thesis statements)

Ability to draw conclusions
(rather than merely summarize discussion)

Applications and practical implications (where relevant)

Further topics of study identified

Now, I realize that before writing a paper, you really don't know what to think about the material. But writing a conclusion early is still useful. It won't be a final, perfect version. Write out a version that reflects what you think and know now. This version should provoke you to think about these various issues early in the process and reveal what the body of your paper must accomplish.

Doing this early in your seminary career will help you understand the process by breaking it into distinct steps. As you do this more and more you won't need to write everything out. I'll admit, I don't always write out an outline. And I very rarely write an introduction before I start researching and as far as I know I've never written a conclusion before I've finished writing the paper. However, and this is a big however, after writing so many papers over the years I have all these issues in my head, so that even if I'm not writing, I'm thinking in the terms I've shown you. I think of all the various topics, goals, and priorities and what matters.

I'm had students do this in my intro classes so that they are pushed to think about these issues as well. In future classes, you may or may not follow the pattern I'm setting for you here. You might very well, write an introduction, a body, and a conclusion in one massive exertion of energy. Do what works best for you.

However, what you will always have to do is keep all these issues in mind along the way, organizing your study either on paper or in your head, so that the actual process of writing isn't about filling up a blank canvas. I'm teaching you how to color by numbers here. Makes for a much easier process and generally a much better paper.

# Time, Life, and the Temptations

I want to take another reflection break in the midst of our academic discussion of theological studies. Despite what the title of this chapter sounds like, this isn't an advertisement for a collection of songs from one of the most popular Motown groups in history.

This is about the struggles of seminary and an encouragement to learn how to make your way through it as an integrated person.

It's so easy to compartmentalize our lives, to have our family section, our work section, our school section, our spiritual section, our fun section. The trouble comes when these different sections are not just different parts of our lives, but become separated topics. But, the human psyche doesn't work well under those conditions. As much as we'd like to compartmentalize, one compartment influences another. And we get burned out if we see one area being purely about an external task, without palpable contributions to our lives.

In the study of theology and in the activities of ministry, our spirituality becomes work rather than renewal, a task to get done rather than a feast to celebrate.

With that in mind, here's some thoughts from Paul's letter to the Philippians:

> **3:1 Further, my brothers and sisters, rejoice in the Lord! It is no trouble for me to write the same things to you again, and it is a safeguard for you. 2 Watch out for those dogs, those evildoers, those mutilators of the flesh. 3 For it is we who are the circumcision, we who serve God by his Spirit, who boast in Christ Jesus, and who**

put no confidence in the flesh— 4 though I myself have reasons for such confidence.

If someone else thinks they have reasons to put confidence in the flesh, I have more: 5 circumcised on the eighth day, of the people of Israel, of the tribe of Benjamin, a Hebrew of Hebrews; in regard to the law, a Pharisee; 6 as for zeal, persecuting the church; as for righteousness based on the law, faultless.

7 But whatever were gains to me I now consider loss for the sake of Christ. 8 What is more, I consider everything a loss because of the surpassing worth of knowing Christ Jesus my Lord, for whose sake I have lost all things. I consider them garbage, that I may gain Christ 9 and be found in him, not having a righteousness of my own that comes from the law, but that which is through faith in Christ—the righteousness that comes from God on the basis of faith. 10 I want to know Christ—yes, to know the power of his resurrection and participation in his sufferings, becoming like him in his death, 11 and so, somehow, attaining to the resurrection from the dead.

12 Not that I have already obtained all this, or have already arrived at my goal, but I press on to take hold of that for which Christ Jesus took hold of me. 13 Brothers and sisters, I do not consider myself yet to have taken hold of it. But one thing I do: Forgetting what is behind and straining toward what is ahead, 14 I press on toward the goal to win the prize for which God has called me heavenward in Christ Jesus.

Pressing on when it seems too hard is the call to each of us. And pressing on is pretty much the main goal of life lived on the Way. Seminary is a wilderness of sorts, a place of testing and challenge and temptation, where we both learn new ways of being but also are tested as to who we are in this moment.

It's easy to become discouraged in the wilderness. There's nothing to eat. There's nothing to drink. The giants in the land are much too big. We think back to earlier days, the time we had and the space, and the seeming freedom in our narrow understanding of the world. Ignorance can very much be bliss. For while at least. But we press forward, not to get the degree, not to put more letters after our name, not to impress friends and family with all the polysyllabic words we know. We press forward to take hold of that for which Christ has taken hold of us.

And one thing you all have in common, which is clear in reading your statements of why you're here in seminary, is that God has taken hold of you so as to deepen you, to train you, to prepare you for leading others in the way of Christ.

Yes, academic life is difficult and often full of obscure topics and difficult readings. Yet, these aren't extraneous to your life with God or your ministry. These aren't the goal, either. Grades aren't the goal. Jumping through the hoops isn't the goal. Even having a properly formatted bibliography isn't the goal. Shocking!

The goal is Christ. And the way, for now, for you, includes this process of study.

There's a lot of really fun facts to learn in seminary and there are a lot of disturbing realities as well. One of these latter isn't as much the topics of our courses as it is the way we respond to strain and stress and struggle.

Our struggle also includes a deepening understanding of God and better capability for ministry, and so there's often an underlying spiritual reality that comes with our mental development.

We're engaged in a spiritual battle, not just an intellectual exercise. Seminary is a place where we learn our strengths, develop our passions, but also, so often, where we encounter our demons -- those personal faults or favored sins or temptations. And often, for many, the bounty of growing in the faith is coupled with a very curious awareness of our faults and failings.

It's easy to ignore or dismiss these as just the static in our life. But, I think that's wrong. Because this is not only a time to learn facts about God, this is a time to hone how we live with God.

In being faced with the temptations in our particular wilderness, we're faced with coming to terms with the spiritual attacks, emotional insecurities, and everything else that will manifest fissures in our future ministries and relationships.

A couple of weeks ago we read about John Wesley, and his amazing ministry. What is curious is how much he struggled personally throughout his life. He had some humbling failures in his first attempt to be a missionary, being kicked out of the colonies with the law close behind him. We heard of his heart being strangely warmed at the Aldersgate meeting, but far too often the quick tellings of that story leave out what comes next in his journals:

"After my return home, I was much buffeted with temptations; but cried out and they fled away. They returned again and again. I as often lifted up my eyes, and He 'sent me help from his holy place.'"

Throughout his ministry he talks about God hiding his face, or being buffeted by many temptations and struggles and frustrations. Yet the key for him, as with Paul and with so many great heroes of the faith, is that they pressed on in the struggles, not letting even their temptations or frustrations hold them back. They continued to cling to God, pressing on towards what was ahead at each step.

This did not mean ignoring their temptations or dismissing them, but rather it meant confronting them in the grace of God, sometimes stumbling, sometimes falling, but always striving to advance, growing deeper and stronger with the struggles, using the tools and the gifts and the hope they had been given to cling to God in the midst of storms and wilderness.

Now is the time to learn how to break down those compartmentalized walls, and discover how to integrate your whole life, so that you're fighting the good fight with a united front. If you see the study of theology or Scripture or spirituality or any of the other topics as areas separate to your own life with God or your ministry, then you're dividing your forces and your attention. In ministry, it is always frustrating to see people doing this, but so often it is the pastor and leaders who are modeling this compartmentalized lifestyle. You have to learn how to be in your life that which you are calling others to be.

You have to learn how to integrate your whole life, so that one area contributes and bolsters the others. When we read theology, we're not just reading words about God, we're trying to come to terms with God, in ways that broadens our understanding and bolsters our hope that God, this God, is the one who orients our whole life.

Theology gives us tools for reflection. We are shown language and learn to discuss issues and how those issues relate to other issues. We're given insight into how the fullness of God relates to the fullness of this world, and our lives in it. We are shown how others in history have responded to the crises, and they become our guides and tutors. But we don't stop with absorbing knowledge for its own sake.

Our life and ministry give us the areas to reflect on. Our life and our training inform each other, giving us depth of insight, not puffing up knowledge, so that we can learn more, each and every day, how to live more in line with the calling of Christ, empowered by the grace of God and the Spirit who frees us to live in a new way.

It is by grace we have been saved, and it is by grace we find more and more integration of this salvation -- this ever deepening salvation -- into our whole lives, in our relationships, in our ministries. This integration frees us to be whole people, no longer slaves to that which tries to distract or dismay us. Remember 2 Corinthians 3!

God is a God who integrates life together, the God who came into this world and lived among us, not limited to particular days, or particular subjects, or compartmentalized topics, or specialized buildings.

So, I encourage you, as you are beginning your studies, to begin to address the challenges and temptations, the temptations towards your favored sins and the temptations to compartmentalize your learning. This is what is meant by pressing on, learning how to be more whole in the midst of a highly fractured world, whole in

Christ, for Christ, with Christ.

That is the prize for which we are being called. And what we are studying now is part of the Way we are being led.

Keep your eyes on the prize. Keep straining for what it ahead.

It is worth it, so worth it.

# Writing a research paper

As I've told students over the years, it's perfectly good and fine that you're struggling while in seminary.

It's not supposed to be easy or obvious. If it was, you wouldn't need to get a degree or take any course. Because it would already be easy and obvious. Indeed, research always has this stretching and strain about it. Your projects and tasks are rightfully a struggle.

One key element to this struggle is realizing that what works in the rest of life doesn't quite work in school. We're using to giving our opinions and thoughts on a subject with this received in an accepting or at least cordial manner. In seminary, you'll find a lot of reminders that you don't know enough, that you're not expressing your thoughts well enough, and all other indicators that your current opinions on a topic do not matter very much to the professor or TA.

It's not that you can't have an opinion or suggestions for improving the Church or theology in your research paper. It's more that you have to put these in the context of why a reader should care what you think.

So what if you have an opinion on this stuff? Lots of people do. What makes your opinions worth listening to? For some people, having the right credentials is enough. Well, you don't have the right credentials for a lot of people at the early stage of seminary. So what is left?

Well, that's where the work of a research paper comes in. You can establish yourself as an authority through research and understanding of the issues involved. You can show a very clear line of reasoning from one position to another and then finding a conclusion arising from this. You make the argument and research provide the basis of your authority, not your opinion. And you have to do so in a way that means I can't just dismiss your opinions out of hand.

Think in these terms (which is a bit harsh): I disagree with your positions on the Lord's supper. Unless you convince me otherwise I will fail you in this class. Just telling me you believe something doesn't matter in this case. Add to this the fact I am a Catholic. Now, I'm really sensitive to mischaracterizing of what I believe.

If this were the case, how will you go about convincing me you are right? You have to both respect the positions you're discussing, and you have to very carefully establish what it is you are trying to get me to agree with. Your thesis is that which you are trying to convince me to believe, and the bulk of your paper is moving me towards that point.

You can add other elements, such as the implications or your own opinions, but you have to be careful to couch those in terms of your own interpretation, not necessarily what the research is proving, if the research hasn't proven it.

Now, of course, that whole setup there is pure fiction, as I don't grade in those terms. But that's a good way to approach a research paper for what is in fact required.

A good thesis comes out of how you are orienting your own understanding of the issues at hand. What is the guiding principle or bit that brings it all together? Or what is the primary lens that you are using to examine it all?

How would you sum up your paper in a sentence, in a way that both gives your conclusion and shows why you went through the work of writing it (rather than just having me read another person's work on the subject)?

What do you think about your topic? Asking that might bring up your answer, and then you'd show why you have that answer, instead of just saying 'just because.'

Far too many research papers boil down to students asserting "just because." That might work in a church or other setting where you have authority to assert your opinion. But it doesn't matter at all in a class. There are times when your opinion is sought or your reflections are asked for. The research paper is not one of those times. You have to show, through your work, why the reader should respect your position and you have to establish why what you think is indeed something worth thinking.

You can't assume we share a common set of beliefs. Nor should you assume that what is self-evident to you actually proven through evidence. You can make assumptions along the way, but you if you do you should say, "this is an assumption." I like to use footnotes for that, saying something like: "although it is outside the scope of this present paper, this is an argued point. I will be assuming this approach in light of preliminary study. For further information see this other work that talks a lot more about it."

So focus. Don't get distracted. And show me, don't just tell me, why I should believe your conclusion. Your assertions of statements are just that, your opinion. But this isn't an opinion paper. It's a research paper. So, support your arguments and lead the reader to your conclusion.

# Why we study theology

A while back, a student posted a response to a rather difficult theology article I required for his class. In his response he questioned the place of theology in our studies. It's a heartfelt response, by a dedicated minister and student, and one that I bet reflects something a lot of you are thinking (but don't want to share with an instructor who is a theologian).

Here's what Joe had to say;

> I kept thinking throughout the reading of this article, when are we going to get to the words: grace and faith. I am finding that sometimes these scholars are looking at issues through a very fine set of glasses and break it down so thoroughly that they forget there is a divine presence of God.

> This statement to me really wrapped up what I thought was being talked about, "The suggestion seems to be that no mere human being can offer an adequate satisfaction for sin by an act of vicarious penitence because no penitential act offered up by a mere human being is sufficient reparation for sin that is infinitely heinous. Instead, God must punish sin in the person of the sinner, or in the person of a vicar, able to offer perfect satisfaction for sin." God chose to give us the vicar who we believe by faith to have given us the grace we will need to enter into eternal glory. Our sin deserves death (whether you compare that to the murderer or the little offense of a brother to a sister). But God ultimately knew this and sent His Son to come down as our atonement for our sins.

To conclude my thoughts, might I ask...why do we feel the need as humans to break down Christianity with a fine toothcomb? Why can't we just read the Bible and apply it to our lives? I know this is a dumb question for a seminary student but I thought I would ask. Since Crisp wrote this article specifically for other theologians to offer their opinions. Does this affect the daily walk of a believer?

I really appreciated his willingness to say all this, because it reflects so much of what new seminary students are thinking, and indeed what so many in the broader church think.

Here's my answer:

"Why can't we just read the Bible and apply it to our lives? I know this is a dumb question for a seminary student but I thought I would ask."

It's not a dumb question. It is a very common question, whether it is explicitly asked or just assumed. It is at the heart of the big division between church and the academy, a big part of why people dismiss theology as being extraneous.

It's also not a dumb question when you take it really seriously as a question.

Why can't we just read the Bible and apply it to our lives? Don't think in general terms or vague exhortations. Wouldn't it be a whole lot easier to read the Bible and apply it to our lives? That would fix the church and our society right there. We would be perfect, no longer sinning, having harmonious relationships with everyone around us, loving our brothers and sisters with a whole, selfless love. We would serve God in every part of our life, starting

71

with our salvation and in the power of the Spirit spreading the Gospel to all people, healing and sharing and living lives free from stress or worry or concern. Why would we fret after all?

Just read it and put it into practice. Why can't we? Do I? Do you?

I won't open up the confessional forum for this course, but I would guess that if I had a confessional, we'd all share ways in which we should have, but didn't put what we know is true into practice. We should, but we can't. Or can we? Romans 8 tells us we are free, no longer slaves to sin. So, why don't we read the Bible and do what it says in every way?

Which raises another question. What did God save us from? Sin, sure, but what is that? Is this something I do, or something I am? If it's something I am, then it doesn't matter what I do, right? If it's something I do, then I need to stop. What if I can't stop? Jesus forgives my sins through his work on the cross, sure, but what about if I sin after I've been baptized?

If I say I love God, but continue to sin, I'm a liar, right? That's what 1 John says. So, am I saved even if I keep sinning or can I sin so much that I lose my salvation? What if I commit the unpardonable sin? What is that anyhow?

And if I'm truly saved by grace, then what's up with all the pressure to evangelize? What if I don't? And does it even matter if God elects people no matter what we, or they, do? Yeah, there's the great commission, but was that for us, or for the disciples?

So, let's assume I am saved from my sin. What does that mean for me today? Does Christ's work on the cross mean that I'm elected as part of God's people and can go on merrily living my life just as everyone else does, happy in the knowledge that when the end comes (is there even an end?) I'll have my ticket punched and get to go with the sheep instead of the goats?

And what's up with that eternal punishment anyhow? Is God really that capricious that based on his whims, some get included and the others amuse him through their eternal suffering? Is God really like Nero?

Anyhow, it doesn't matter. Maybe the Bible is false. Made up stories that mimic all the myths from Babylon onto Rome. Maybe it's really about power and control, religious zealots trying to make everyone do what they want. Think of all the evil that has been caused in the name of Christ.

Weren't the crusaders thinking they were following God's command? The inquisition? Slaves were told that the Bible said they should be content in their slavery. So, Christians think emancipation was wrong, that people should be slaves?

And if Christians can't do what the Bible says, then what's up with the Holy Spirit, who is supposed to give people gifts and talents and empower them for service? Why don't we see healings or miracles, or even just a church that doesn't have gossip or competitions or conflicts?

Why aren't we just Jewish? The Bible tells us that the people of God follow the Law, after all, including all the dietary laws and circumcision. Sure, maybe even if Jesus was the Messiah, he was about fulfilling the Jewish law, not starting a new religion. The whole system got messed up after the Bible was written, maybe.

What's up with the trinity? That's not in the Bible. God is God, but is Jesus? He's a man, right? If he is a man how can he be God too? If he's God, then it's not really fair to compare us to him. Should we try to be like him? Be like Christ? Well, we're not God, so is this possible? How? In what ways was Jesus like God? In what ways can we be?

And this whole issue of end times. Are we just waiting until the end? If God doesn't exist in time, what is the end to him? Does God exist in time? Does God feel the impact of human decisions and human sins? Or is he above it all? If he's above it all, what was the Father experiencing when Jesus was on the cross?

Was Jesus even in pain on the cross? Yeah, but if he's God that doesn't make sense. How does the Father forsake the son, anyhow, aren't they one? And, again, what's up with the Spirit?

And what do we do when we meet together? Sure, we have church services. In their own buildings?! That's not in the Bible. With paid ministers who have special credentials? Should we sing songs? I can't find anything out about that. And who is in charge? Peter was in charge at some point some say, the rock on which the church was built. So, are his successors also in charge? And why does James (who isn't actually named James, his name in the Greek New Testament is Jacob) seem in charge in Acts 15?

Who gets to say who participates in the Lord's Supper? What's the Lord's supper about anyhow? Do we have to be perfect to take it, examining ourselves or risking death? What happens with the bread and wine? This is my body, Jesus said. What does that mean? I mean it's bread, right? Are we cannibals here? It's complicated.

Indeed, apply what to our lives? What matters? Do our bodies matter? What book is the important one? Now, Paul gives those lists of gifts given by the Spirit, which one is mine? How do I use it? Should I?

What if I'm a woman and feel a calling to teach? Paul says women should keep silent, but then commends Priscilla for being a great teacher, and other women as well.

Now, let's say I have a family and I find salvation in Christ. Am I saved for them, so we're all saved together? Or do they have choices of their own? I get baptized (by who? who has that right to baptize me?), and my wife does, but does my 10 year old (assuming I have one), does my seven day old?

I could go on...

Theology matters because we do have the Bible but we don't have a systematic set of exactly what to believe on every question and what we should do in every situation. Change that. The Law in the early parts of the Old Testament is extremely detailed, and gives us all sorts of guidelines. But, we say we don't need to follow that anymore.

So what do we do? How should we live? How should we gather? What does the Bible actually teach? Who gets to decide who is right if we disagree about what the Bible teaches?

That's the thing with theology. It developed over the course of centuries as real Christians asked pressing questions and wrestled with difficult answers.

We might have the same questions asked of us or might have new questions. How do we respond in a way that is the most faithful to the whole testimony of Scripture and revelation?

Which leads to the second part of your question:

"Since Crisp wrote this article specifically for other theologians to offer their opinions. Does this affect the daily walk of a believer?"

You note "a believer". Who? I mean specifically. Are you talking about yourself or someone in your community? Are you asking if this affects Crisp personally (or are you assuming he's not a believer?).

What about less forensic oriented cultures, who are more concerned about shame than legal status? Do we have to convert them first to understanding the nature of a penal system? What about Jewish men and women?

How about our image of God? Now is God a stern judge who seeks everyone's damnation unless we grovel and plead? Is he looking to save people, or is he wary of that? Is God a judge or is he a father? What kind of Father uses courtroom imagery for dealing with disobedient children?

But, I'll come back to "a believer." That's a general concept that's not very helpful because 'a believer' doesn't actually exist.

Does this article help you? It sounds like you're having trouble applying this to your life.

What about me? I will be honest in saying that for me, growing up in a very Evangelical, very evangelistic, setting where the whole of the Gospel was about getting people into the club, that I was well on my way of losing my faith because the very shallow answers of a mostly middle-class religion oriented towards assuaging the guilt of existential angst had very little to say to me when we lost our home when I was 8 and even as I prayed and prayed and prayed as a young boy, life just was one struggle after another. More homes were lost, food was often scarce. My mom's massive medical problems undermined my family's attempts to move forward financially.

Was I being punished for my sins? Was my mom being punished when, despite being absolutely faithful to God, she got polio when she was 3, and then experienced the crushing emotional and physical pain when she was in her 40s.

Churches had absolutely nothing to say to me during these crises.Because my walk had very little to do with their very limited perception of the generalized "Christian". Or the answer they had for that nonspecific "believer," the one who is supposed to ask all the questions they give in evangelism or apologetics books and be satisfied by the answers.

And so my reading of history and theology became my lifeline to the deeper reality, in all its fullness, of the Christian faith, which wasn't about providing a generalized answers to generalized questions, but was about a living relationship with an infinitely complex God who sought to raise me, even me, up out of my frustrations and sins, and point me to a new way of life, a life lived in the power of the Spirit.

What does that mean for me today? Does questions of Christ's work on the cross, and what happened and why, have an affect on me? Yes. Because how God works says a lot about who God is, and who God is says a lot about how this world is.

What difference does it make specifically? Well, you'd have to be specific in telling the story of a particular Christian.

What difference does it make to have a stern, legal, unattached Judge in charge of salvation to a woman who had an authoritarian father, who beat her unless she did everything perfect and cowed before his rage?

Or what does it mean to a person who really has messed up a whole lot in life, who gets how they were put straight and helped towards living right by a legal system that punished but also rehabilitated them?

The latter accepts God, because he gets that imagery. The former rejects God because God sounds too much like the evil father she only now is barely moving beyond.

Is God unable to save that woman because she rejects the imagery that is popular in evangelism? Or does the cross mean something to her too? Is she wrong, and not saved, if she finds Christ in the light of a different, more palatable, image of the cross? This might be one that addresses her understood need for salvation, a salvation from brokenness and darkness, rather than assuaging existential guilt.

Where was God in the holocaust? Was that judgment upon the stubborn Jews for not accepting the work of the cross? Is salvation just a moral thing? Or is it also physical and emotional? What about those who aren't healed, or who continue to sin?

What does it mean for me for me to respond to others as Christ did to me? How we understand the work of the cross radically affects how we understand God, how we understand salvation, how we understand sin, and thus how we, each in our particular way, come to terms with our memories, our experiences, and our calling on this day.

Do you get what I'm doing here? I'm pushing back hard, but not because I deny the validity of your questions. It's precisely because it's a good question, a question so many are asking, and we all will continue to ask at points in our education and ministries.

Theology is much more than having a set of facts about God, serving as a checklist of right beliefs for us to be fully approved members of the club. Theology affects us because our understanding of God affects how we live, and because no one has the same experiences or the same responses to imagery or the same priorities or questions, we can't talk about the general "believer" but have to be aware that Christ came to save specific people, who have their own specific questions and fears and hurts and hopes.

Having a breadth of theological knowledge means we're not limited to a very narrow range of questions or lifestyles. The Church has been very good about reaching out to middle and upper middle class people precisely because it has maintained a narrow theology that is able to respond to the common questions of this group.

That's why so many fall away, however. Why there is a major exodus from the church during college years. Because once people realize that life isn't so neatly packaged, and there are major challenges to the assumptions of the faith, and it really is true that for the most part Christians either can't or won't do what the Bible says, then what's the point of getting up on a Sunday morning or believing in what to all appearances seems a fantasy myth for insecure people?

Theology, then, is a way of gathering resources and understanding about God, getting to know God from his own revelation and from friends of his who have known him over the years. This means that when we interact with specific people, who have specific issues, we're not limited to a sales script about God's benefits, accessories or attributes.

We're able to interact with them on a highly varied basis, giving an answer for the hope that is in us, sharing with them the hope that can redeem their pasts, in an always flexible, always creative, always unique way. We get to know God, and in knowing God more and more, we are able to share the fullness of his truth in manifold ways, in ways that affects the walk of each specific believer, no matter where they are starting from and no matter what they are experiencing.

Because we testify that God is not limited to only a narrow range of experiences or backgrounds.

Does an academic theology article affect your walk with God? Well, probably their answers and the questions really do affect it more than you think, and certainly affect the lives of others who are seeking salvation from something or someone. How does it affect it specifically?

Well, that's the pastoral question, the question that is answered through prayer, discernment, and, yes, pastoral training, so that we who read such theology, who also read Scripture, can apply the fullness of truth to the specifics of real people's lives.

That's the calling, I think, of a pastor.

# Theology and Ministry

I like it when students post a heartfelt question or struggle in forums. It gives me a sense of their experience. I don't reply to every student post, but I like to reply to the bigger picture comments because I realize that the student posting is not alone. Here's something a student wrote in a forum on the topic of theology and I think it's worth noting, because I totally agree in part and think it's highly relevant to any discussion of theological studies. Have a read:

> I will admit, I am not the biggest fan of theology, everyone has it, we all use it, it is necessary, but I am still not the biggest fan. This article, and Patrick's testimony does give me some more appreciation for theology but it will take time for me to truly appreciate all of theology. From my experience I have seen theology in a lot of ways like an automobile. Everyone uses them to get where they are going whether they know much about how the automobile works or not. But for the most part when I see discussions of theology it seems to be a lot like someone showing off their sports car and bashing their neighbors broken down Junker.
>
> Instead of stopping by and helping their neighbor get to the next destination by offering assistance in helping to fix their car (or introducing them to the mechanic that actually can fix the car). Whether that illustration makes sense or not what I am trying to say is that I have seen a lot of Bible battles that yield few results. No one is won over by being whipped down intellectually, which is why relational ministry and discipleship is a preferred alternative to intellectual debate.

I'll admit here that what the student says above is indeed true.

There's a lot of reasons not to like theology, and most of those reasons have to do with how other people use theology to cause problems, or make divisions, or beat down others, or try to raise themselves up.

In theology and ministry both there's a common tendency to try to beat out others, to assume power, to want to show how smart, or talented or hardworking you are. All too often these approaches come out of a person's ego, trying to gain confidence in what they are doing, trying to prove themselves to others, rather than gaining their confidence in God.

The sad fact is that far too often these dysfunctional ways of approaching theology make it so that men and women are turned off by reading theology, because they have been shown or taught there's only a certain way of approaching theology.

The same is true for ministry. People are turned off pursuing God not because they don't like God for who he is, but because they don't like God for how his supposed people have presented him.

Which is a shame.

Now this week as we engage the topics of ministry it might be easy to think that we left behind the more academic topics of the past, the classroom and library work, and now are finally getting to the practical stuff. Only that's not the case.

Everything we've done so far is absolutely related to the stuff we're studying this week. The stronger your foundation in each of those previous topics, the stronger you will be in your ministry.

Each element feeds into the topics of discernment, preaching, understanding your context, understanding a vision for your community, and everything else. The trouble is that because we think theology is this one thing and ministry is something entirely different, we ignore helpful tools that will give us a stronger ministry in whatever setting.

Here's the trick: Don't let anyone else tell you how theology must be done. Don't use theology to beat down others, don't use it to make yourself seem smarter, don't get puffed up by the knowledge, use theology to help you understand yourself, and God, and how you help others see God.

Even if others are using theology poorly, don't get discouraged by their misuse. Make your own way with it.

The fact is that how we understand God affects how we lead, how we preach, how we encourage others, how we caution others. What we believe about God shapes every part of our responses in this life, and so having a ever sharpening understanding of God and his work in this world will radically shape who you are as a minister, whether you minister vocationally or not.

Relational ministry and discipleship are entirely theological tasks, as we are making relationships with each other and God, so it would seem quite important to learn more about who God is. Only because we are told theology is only intellectual, it seems distant.

It is up to us, however, to help overcome this distortion, first for ourselves and then for others, because maturity in Christ and becoming disciples is a holistic task. What we think about God affects how we respond, and how we respond affects what we think.

Theology is a reflection on the practices, and the practices give us guidance to steer our reflections.
Trying to go drive somewhere we've never been is almost impossible if you don't have a map or directions. Sure you might find it by trial and error, but that takes so much more time and you'll almost certainly get lost for at least a little while. But just having a map or directions is useless if we don't get in the car and actually drive to the destination.

So, this process of education isn't just about getting the extraneous stuff done so that you can get on with the business of ministry. Indeed, most of you are already in that business.

At each step, think about what the underlying theology is and how it fits with what is in Scripture, what is in Christian history, what has been developed as people reflect on God over the centuries in a more systematic way.

Think about your situations so that what you do, how you respond, how you pray, how you encourage and build up others, isn't just a managerial task but truly reflects the fullness and depths of the Kingdom of God.

It's God's calling to us, after all, so let us be faithful in this task, not letting the sin and distortions of others pull us away from what are wonderful insights and helpful maps for our efforts.

And in all of this, let us stay in tune with the Spirit, for only with God and through God can we experience God in our life and with others.

Made in United States
Troutdale, OR
12/15/2024

26505529R00053